S. A. S.

SINGLE AND SATISFIED

BY PENNY L. GRACE

S.A.S.: Single and Satisfied

Trilogy Christian Publishers A Wholly Owned Subsidiary of Trinity Broadcasting Network

2442 Michelle Drive Tustin, CA 92780

Copyright © 2022 by Penny L. Grace

Scripture quotations marked NASB are taken from the New American Standard Bible® (NASB), Copyright © 1960, 1962, 1963, 1968, 1971, 1972, 1973, 1975, 1977, 1995 by The Lockman Foundation. Used by permission. www.Lockman.org. Scripture quotations marked NIV are taken from the Holy Bible, New International Version®, NIV®. Copyright © 1973, 1978, 1984, 2011 by Biblica, Inc.TM Used by permission of Zondervan. All rights reserved worldwide. www.zondervan.com. The "NIV" and "New International Version" are trademarks registered in the United States Patent and Trademark Office by Biblica, Inc.TM Scripture quotations marked NLT are taken from the Holy Bible, New Living Translation, copyright © 1996, 2004, 2015 by Tyndale House Foundation. Used by permission of Tyndale House Publishers, Inc., Carol Stream, Illinois 60188. All rights reserved. Scripture quotations marked NKJV are taken from the New King James Version®. Copyright © 1982 by Thomas Nelson. Used by permission. All rights reserved. Scripture quotations marked KJV are taken from the King James Version of the Bible. Public domain.

No part of this book may be reproduced, stored in a retrieval system, or transmitted by any means without written permission from the author. All rights reserved. Printed in the USA.

Rights Department, 2442 Michelle Drive, Tustin, CA 92780.

Trilogy Christian Publishing/TBN and colophon are trademarks of Trinity Broadcasting Network.

Cover design by: Natalee Dunning

For information about special discounts for bulk purchases, please contact Trilogy Christian Publishing.

Trilogy Disclaimer: The views and content expressed in this book are those of the author and may not necessarily reflect the views and doctrine of Trilogy Christian Publishing or the Trinity Broadcasting Network.

Manufactured in the United States of America

10 9 8 7 6 5 4 3 2 1

Library of Congress Cataloging-in-Publication Data is available.

ISBN: 978-1-68556-290-8

E-ISBN: 978-1-68556-291-5

*Satisfied in Who God Created Me to Be,
Just Me, Loving Unconditionally.*

"The Book"

For many years God would send people, even strangers, to me with the message "write the book." I am so glad that God did. So, this is "the book" that God wanted me to write. I pray that each person has a wonderful personal experience and encounter with God while reading it. I sure did!

Love and blessings,
Penny L. Grace

Dedication

I lovingly dedicate this labor of love to Jesus. Thank you, Jesus, for the price You paid by giving Your life on Calvary to redeem God's people back to Him. Yes, thank You, Jesus, for death and resurrection. You are truly my Hero. Thank You, Jesus, for not giving up on me and continuously encouraging and pushing me to write this book. So, for You, Jesus, I wrote this book. I love You with all my heart and with all my soul and with all my mind. Jesus, You are my Strength, You are my Fortress, and I am forever Your Servant and Apostle.

Penny L. Grace

Table of Contents

My Mother's Heart Shared i
Foreword iii
Introduction v
Can Money or Things Fill My Void? 1
Am I Single? 3
Am I Single? 5
"Faith and Hope" 7
Single Defined 9
The Joy of the Lord 11
What's Missing in My Life? 15
Single by a Separation 17
Single by Widowhood 19
Attitudes 21
Attitudes (An Attitude of Gratitude) 25
Mary: Attitude of Faith and Acceptance 27
Single After a Divorce 29
Single After a Divorce 31
Is Separation the Same as Divorce? 33
Am I There Yet? (Different Types of Love) 35
What's Love Got to Do with It? 37
How I Learned to Love Again after a Divorce 39
How I Learned to Love Again after a Divorce 41

Single and Waiting for a Husband	43
Single and Waiting for a Wife	45
Feeling Single and Alone after the Death of a Child (A Parent's Devastation)	47
Feeling Single and Aloneafter the Death of a Child (A Parent's Devastation)	49
I Am Born Again/a Believer, Now What?	51
A Queen-Vashti Attitude?	53
Just This, That and All the Rest	55
Overcoming Times of Frustration	57
Who Can I Talk to, and How Can They Help Me?	59
Married but Single	61
Single and Pregnant	63
Knowledge	67
Wisdom	69
Wisdom and Knowledge Together	71
Why Do I Need to BeBorn Again (Saved)?	73
Forgiveness/Unforgiveness	75
A Special Invitation	77
My Personal Deliverance by God from My Adversary	79
My Personal Deliverance by God from My Adversary (Continued)	83
My Personal Deliverance by God from My Adversary (Continued)	85
Encouraging Scripturesto Read Daily	87
About the Author	89

My Mother's Heart Shared

This treasure that you have decided to read will be a blessing to your life. There are times when we have to take a look at ourselves and do an inventory from the inside out, not from the outside in. Sometimes being thankful for where we are in our lives is a hard thing to do. Maybe we think we are not where we feel we should be at this point in our lives, or maybe it could be that we are constantly comparing our lives to others.

To be content with the person you are and where you are in life is a daily challenge. Change only comes after you are thankful for what you have right now. I assure you that after reading this book, you will have a better outlook on being single and satisfied with just who God has created and formed you to be. You will learn how to love yourself after realizing what a treasure you are and how much the Lord loves you. *Single and Satisfied* will forever change your inner being to be able to accept whatever comes your way by trusting God for everything and in everything.

Pastor Eric M. Neely Sr.
AMP Church, Burlington, NC

Foreword

"You better check for worms." Those are the words of my dear grandmother, Rosa Sellars Highsmith. As a child, I liked apples. Often I would approach the family apple tree, grab an apple to eat, and each time that I was about to eat it without inspection or cleansing, my grandmother would intercept my actions. You see, she had the wisdom to check for worms before biting into it. Because of my youth, I would bite the apple first, only to find that the apple, which I so desired, was contaminated by worms.

In relationships, many of us are biting apples to check for worms when it is not necessary. Each time I found an apple that I desired, it appeared to look good at first glance. However, after the first bite, I would experience disappointment and brokenness, but eventually, Grandmother taught me how to select apples without biting into them.

I am honored to write this foreword in Apostle Penny Grace's book, titled *Single and Satisfied*. Many who may choose to read this book may be experiencing challenges in their lives due to failed relationships. Unfortunately, I understand because I have personally experienced the ugly thing called "divorce." Even though I have been married most of my adult life, I still remember the seasons of singleness, times of hurt, bitterness, and loneliness.

This book is so important. I believe that it will refresh many, encourage most, give hope to some, give answers to a few, but help all who are single at this time for whatever reason. By the time you finish reading this book, you will no longer walk in brokenness. Penny's book will lead to a place of completeness through Christ and not a person. She will teach you how to fill the void in your life with the proper driving force, which is your relationship with Jesus Christ. For those of you who are suffering and grieving stemming from the loss of a loved one, you also will discover how to recover from your loss and become healed from your brokenness.

This book is a "must" read. It is informative and challenging. The writings will equip you to be content in a state of singleness without feeling that life is over! You will be inspired. I take this opportunity to congratulate Penny on a job well done!

Bishop Lorenzo N. Peterson, DTh
Author of The Pathway to Perfection
Spanaway, Washington

Introduction

Practically every little girl and numerous little boys dream of growing up, getting married, and having a family. Yes, we must admit that there are more little girls than little boys with this dream, but one thing is for sure: no child dreams of being single for the rest of his or her life. Children will create invisible playmates so that they'll have someone to play with or talk to and keep them company. This "emotional security blanket" shows that there is something within us, something that moves us to a desire of not being alone. We like and enjoy friendship and fellowship with each other. We want a friend, someone to play with and talk to, even as very young children. We want to feel loved, be loved, and to love.

Maybe at one point in every person's life, she or he will feel content in dating more than one person or just enjoying her or his single life for a while until that one very special person comes along. Then, even though you used to enjoy your own company and solitude, you become willing to open your world to include this special person—yes, that one special breathtaking individual who you thought never existed.

I haven't met that special man yet, but I know that one day I will, and this encounter will require me to write another book (smile). However, until God brings him into my life, I will continue to be single and satisfied, satisfied with God being my everything. Jesus says in Matthew 12:50 (KJV), "For whosoever shall do the will of my Father which is in heaven, the same is my brother, and sister, and mother." I have learned how to be satisfied with the very ones that God has put in my life. You, dear reader, must learn to do likewise. I realized that being single means just that, "single." You must be happy with just who you are and with how God created and made you. Meanwhile, be content with God being everything you need in life until that one special "person" is placed in front of you. Then your eyes will be opened, and finally, you will realize that what you see is what God has placed in your life. When it's time to marry, get beside this person, and walk together as one "until death do you part." Even after meeting that "one God has chosen for you," you will still need to be happy with the person you are.

"Single" is not a bad thing at all. "Single" is a "whole" thing: meaning that in order to be happy with whom you are, you must first learn to be single and satisfied, with whom God created you to be, to love unconditionally.

In this book, I will be sharing my experiences in life and how my relationship with the Lord encourages me on a daily basis, allows me to come through many bad times, hard times, even tragic incidents, and enables me to overcome them all by the power of God. In this book, you will find many addressed "helps" and "questions" answered. This will not be a typical chapter-by-chapter book. This will be an experience-with-the-Lord book. For this is "the book."

Topics and chapters will be here and there, not in an orderly matter, but then we must realize that that's how things come to us in life.

So, get ready to experience the Lord, as I did in writing this book and was being led by the Holy Spirit. Keep your mind, heart, ears, and eyes open, and be sensitive to the imperative information and godly wisdom as told to me by the Lord. This will not be just a "good read," but also a "good source of information" that you can use on your daily walk during your life here on earth: wisdom beyond my understanding and ability to give to people. Wisdom will be shared that everyone will know, without a doubt, has come from the Lord. That's one of the reasons that this book took over three years to complete. Just like our God, this book will have no beginning and no end. You will be able to pick up this book, start reading from any page and get information, direction, instruction, and prayers to follow on a daily basis.

This book (S.A.S.) is for the believer and unbeliever, with hopes and prayers that the unbeliever will become a believer in Christ. Everyone who is single needs to be single and satisfied. Godly wisdom is needed by every living being because God created every living creature. The Bible tells us in Genesis 1:27 (NKJV), "So God created man in His *own* image; in the image of God He created him; male and female He created them." Please notice that it's stated in the Bible "that God created male and female." No matter what is said, told, exaggerated, suggested, or believed, God created "male and female."

No one or anything on this earth will be able to recreate man or woman again. God is the only "Creator." Satan can use a man or woman to try to change or alter God's creation, but never will man or woman be able to create a "living being" from the ground/dirt or from a "rib," as God has already perfectly done.

Love and blessings,
Penny L. Grace

Can Money or Things Fill My Void?

That answer is very easy to bring to a conclusion: "*No*." If money could make you happy and fill that empty void, then why do wealthy individuals take their lives and leave all those things and money behind? Money will only complicate life for you if you are not "whole" before you come into that money. Remember that you can always be born into money and live a very lonely life. Certain celebrities must keep their children isolated and hidden away so that the electronic media and tabloids will not hurt and exploit them, but at one point, even in the lives of those children, they, too, must come face-to-face with their own feelings, choices and the lives they will have to choose and live for themselves.

No one can be hidden from reality forever. At one point in your life, you will have to make a decision to either have your own personal relationship with the Lord or deny Him. I caution you with what Jesus says in Matthew 10:33 (KJV), "But whosoever denies Me before men, him I will also deny before My Father which is in heaven."

One of the most wonderful truths that I like about the Word of God is that no matter what you believe, whether God is real, Jesus is real, the devil is real, angels are real or not, it does not change what God says and who God is. He is the God of all the earth: "For God is the King of all the earth; sing to him a psalm of praise" (Psalm 47:7, NIV). He is the "I Am." I love what God told Moses in Exodus 3:14 (NIV): "God said to Moses, 'I AM

WHO I AM. This is what you are to say to the Israelites: 'I AM has sent me to you.'" Wow, how I love God! I truly thank God for who He is and for my Lord and Savior Jesus Christ, and for the Holy Spirit that resides in me, dwells in me, and leads and guides me in my daily walk of salvation here on earth.

Things are just that, "things." Things are earthly stuff that you can't take with you to your grave. Things and/or money will never fill a void in your life. Only the one who created you can do that. If you have already tried everything known to you with no success, why not try Jesus?

Oh, just let me take a quick praise break right here and shout "Hallelujah" to God's Holy name. Whew, I sure hope you took a praise break with me because it really was good!

Am I Single?

Being single is a mindset and decision that needs to be made from your inner being and not a decision resulting from past or present hurts. Being single should be a decision made by a healthy individual, not a broken person or circumstance. You must always remember that a single day can change your entire life. You may be feeling one way right now, but tomorrow can bring your miracle, your answered prayer, and/or your blessings. Just take one day at a time. Don't try to live an entire week, month, or year in one day. Don't make a life decision dependent upon a moment of crisis. God brought me through, and He will do the same for you. Don't give up, and stay prayed up until God calls you up. As long as your eyes are closed, you will see only darkness, but once you allow God to open your eyes that you might see, then you will then see the light that He has sent into this world to bring light to every dark place and situation in your life.

Be encouraged by John 3:16–21:

> For God so loved the world that he gave his one and only Son, that whoever believes in him shall not perish but have eternal life. For God did not send his Son into the world to condemn the world, but to save the world through him. Whoever believes in him is not condemned, but whoever does not believe stands condemned already because they have not believed in the name of God's one and only Son. This is the verdict: Light has come into the world, but people loved

> darkness instead of light because their deeds were evil. Everyone who does evil hates the light, and will not come into the light for fear that their deeds will be exposed. But whoever lives by the truth comes into the light, so that it may be seen plainly that what they have done has been done in the sight of God.
>
> John 3:16–21 (NIV)

Jesus is the light of the world, so once you accept Jesus as your Savior, then His light will shine through all the darkness in this world and in your daily life. You will be able to see things in the marvelous light of Jesus. He will shine through your everyday trials and tribulations.

So many things come from our daily walk of life, and we need Jesus to be with us to help us walk through them daily. He did it for me, and I know He is willing to do it for you if you just open your mouth and give Him your heart today. Being single is a beautiful feeling and time of your life just to learn and enjoy yourself daily. Every day is a gift from God to us, and we should live and enjoy every day, as tomorrow is not promised to any of us.

James 4:14 (NIV) reminds us, "Why, you do not even know what will happen tomorrow. What is your life? You are a mist that appears for a little while and then vanishes." Therefore, if we are not promised tomorrow, then why worry about tomorrow, which may never come. It's great to plan for your future and the future of your loved ones as well, but don't try to take away tomorrow when you are not sure it will come, and even if it does come, then it can always be better than your today.

Am I Single?

Remember that no matter how bad it is or how bad it hurts, or especially how embarrassing you might think something will be, it can all change in one second. Life is all about changes. Embrace change instead of fearing or fighting it. Sometimes it may feel as if your life is falling apart when what is really happening is that your life is being put in place by God. Trust Him, for He is the One who created you and knows what's best for you. Ponder the following, and be consoled as you await your breakthrough:

"'For I know the plans I have for you,' declares the LORD, 'plans to prosper you and not to harm you, plans to give you hope and a future'" (Jeremiah 29:11, NIV).

"Faith and Hope"

The Bible tells us in Hebrews 11:1 (NIV), "Now faith is confidence in what we hope for and assurance about what we do not see." Therefore, we must always try to keep our hope no matter what.

Even if you get married, there is no guarantee that you will be together for the rest of your life, but if you have been born again, then you will find hope in your "faith in God" and His Word, which tells us, "What God has put together let no man put asunder," meaning that when you wait on the Lord, I mean truly be obedient and wait on the Lord and who He has chosen for you, no man, woman, or thing will be able to separate you if you keep Jesus in the middle of your relationship.

We must always keep growing in love and showing unconditional love for each other. Let us not be found judging, ruling, or holding onto things of the past that have hurt or wronged us, but may we be found releasing an unconditional love in our lives and nurturing relationships that can come only from God through His Holy Spirit (unconditional love).

A relationship/marriage, just like God's Word, is conditional, even though God's love for His people is unconditional. Put another way, He will not leave us but will allow us to leave Him or His will if that's what we decide to do. God will not touch our "free will." God will never take control of our free will and make us do what He wants us to do; if so, then we would be like robots, and that is not His will for His creations. We must choose to do right versus wrong. We, as His creation, must choose for ourselves whom we will serve: God, Satan, man, woman, child/children, money—whatever we choose. But beware because you will surely live out your choice, and it could cost you your life and relationship with the One who created you, God (Joshua 24:15).

Remember that what you are going through does not define who you are or how your life will be. It's just for a moment, and then things will always change if you are willing to "change."

Prayer: God, please help my faith and hope to be renewed as I read this book and in every day of my life. I need changes in my life, so I am looking to You to lead and guide me daily by your Spirit. In Jesus' name, I pray, Amen!

Single Defined

First, let's take a deep look at what being single means. "Single" means a lot of different things to different people. For instance, the word "single" defined by Webster has many definitions, such as "not married, unaccompanied by others," and a few others, but the most impacting definition to me is as follows: "Consisting of a separate unique whole."

You have to be "whole" before you can "divide" or "share" yourself with anyone in any way. Knowing and believing that we were created by God to love and be loved, there will always be a void until you find that love or way of feeling totally loved, which can come only from our Creator and Maker, God, our Father, the only Creator and Maker of all creation.

The type of single that I am talking about in this book is the single that every individual must have, whether married, single, separated, divorced, or engaged. You must be single in your relationship with God. You came into this world naked and covered with particles from inside of your mother's womb. Even with twins, they only come out one at a time. Two children are not taken out of the mother together. Likewise, in life, your relationship with God needs to be as a single individual first, then with your spouse. If you are not happy single, you will never be happy married. No one should control your happiness. Happiness comes from within; it is rooted deep down and will not be contingent upon anyone other than yourself. You must also have the *joy* of the Lord. What is the *joy* of the Lord? Continue reading this book, and you will find out.

The Joy of the Lord

What is the joy of the Lord, and how do I get it?

Joy comes from the Lord. In the Bible, James 1:2–4 says,

> Consider it pure joy, my brothers and sisters, whenever you face trials of many kinds, because you know that the testing of your faith produces perseverance. Let perseverance finish its work so that you may be mature and complete, not lacking anything.
>
> James 1:2–4 (NIV)

One reading this would think this does not make sense, "humanly." How and why would you be joyful when you're going through hard times or when bad things happen to you? That just does not make any sense! That's why we need to give our hearts to Jesus. Because we will never fully understand what the Word of God says or the mind of God until we look at it through the eyes of God. Learning to respond with joy during times of tragedy or just hard times in life must begin with a true awareness that God really is at work in our lives, that God has a purpose for what we are experiencing, and that God will bring you through it all.

God alone can produce true joy, and He does that naturally through His Spirit living in those who have put their life and trust in Him. It's important for us to understand that only God Himself can give us the ability to respond to life's difficult circumstances with that inner contentment and satisfaction.

"But the Holy Spirit produces this kind of fruit in our lives: love, joy, peace, patience, kindness, goodness, faithfulness, gentleness, and self-control. There is no law against these things!" (Galatians 5:22–23, NLT)

The joy of the Lord is deep-rooted. He gives you a joy that is unspeakable, a joy that overflows, a joy that keeps you going in spite of "difficult times" in your life and in this world. It's always there, no matter what happens. It's a blessed assurance that no matter what you're going through or what happens, God got you, and He will not only bring you out but walk with you through it and help this to strengthen you in areas of your life that you were originally weak and afraid to go through. Joy is an outpouring of the Holy Spirit. Joy comes from our choices to choose joy. You must choose joy, not wait until something happen, then go look for it. Joy is there before anything happens to you. Joy is a choice. The Bible says in Habakkuk 3:18 (KJV), "Yet I will rejoice in the LORD, I will joy in the God of my salvation." Also, in Psalm 35:9 (KJV), "And my soul shall be joyful in the LORD: it shall rejoice in his salvation." Then Jesus says in John 15:11 (NKJV), "These things I have spoken to you, that My joy may remain in you, and *that* your joy may be full." Get full of Jesus, and you will be full of His "joy."

Prayer: Father God, I desire to have Your joy in my life, so I am asking You to allow me to feel Your joy that I may be able to live the full life that Jesus came that I may have in abundance. Allow Your Spirit to produce this joy in my inner me, deep-rooted, that I may walk in Your strength and no longer in mine daily, especially during my trials and tribulations on this earth. In Jesus' name, I pray, Amen!

I encourage you that you can do this by the Holy Spirit, which you received when you accepted Jesus as Lord and Savior of your life.

Remember Galatians 5:25 (NIV), "Since we live by the Spirit, let us keep in step with the Spirit."

What's Missing in My Life?

Only the real baker knows what's in his/her cake. So, if someone tasting the cake says, "Oh, I like it, but it tastes tangy," only the baker will know the cause of that "tangy" taste, and then he/she will know what needs to be omitted the next time when baking this cake. Likewise, only our Creator knows what He put in us and what we need to be fed to keep us moving in life.

Sometimes, things or circumstances in life will separate us from our loved ones. This is a very unique place to be. You're not divorced, but you're not married. So, what am I? You are not at the beginning, but also are not at the end, just in-between: in-between being married and divorced. You will find yourself asking question after question after question. But that's okay because the Word of God has all the answers you need and want to live a healthy life right here on earth.

During a separation, why not take this time to work on your own personal relationship with God, as I did. I realized that I had forgotten about myself and my likes/dislikes. I had poured myself into my marriage, my ministry, and my family so deeply (trying to be there for everyone all the time) that I had not allowed myself to be ministered to while ministering to others. It is possible to be so involved in ministry, family, and ministering to others that you forget about yourself. You can get so busy helping others that you fail to realize your need to help yourself. You are actually missing "you" and "your" needs. At one point, just before the crucial moment of giving His life for us (redemption), Jesus actually prays for Himself:

> After Jesus said this, he looked toward heaven and prayed: 'Father, the hour has come. Glorify your Son, that your Son may glorify you. For you granted him authority over all people that he might give eternal life to all those you have given him. Now this is eternal life: that they know you, the only true God, and Jesus Christ, whom you have sent. I have brought you glory on earth by finishing the work you gave me to do. And now, Father, glorify me in your presence with the glory I had with you before the world began.'
>
> John 17:1–5 (NIV)

Then Jesus goes on and prays for His disciples and for even us (all believers).

> 'My prayer is not for them alone. I pray also for those who will believe in me through their message, that all of them may be one, Father, just as you are in me and I am in you. May they also be in us so that the world may believe that you have sent me. I have given them the glory that you gave me, that they may be one as we are one—I in them and you in me—so that they may be brought to complete unity. Then the world will know that you sent me and have loved them even as you have loved me. Father, I want those you have given me to be with me where I am, and to see my glory, the glory you have given me because you loved me before the creation of the world. Righteous Father, though the world does not know you, I know you, and they know that you have sent me. I have made you known to them, and will continue to make you known in order that the love you have for me may be in them and that I myself may be in them.'
>
> John 17:20–26 (NIV)

Single by a Separation

"Separation," what does it mean? One of the definitions that Webster has for "separation" is "to sever contractual relations with…"

During the "single" phase that I am going through, I realize that this is the perfect time to get to know God. It's the perfect time to get to know me. What do I like? Do I like movies or live shows? Do I like staying at home or going out? What do I really like, and who am I? Am I an introvert or an extrovert? What are my favorite colors and why? What shows do I enjoy, and what shows do I not like? Am I a morning person or a night owl?

Sometimes we get so tied up in relationships or marriages that we allow ourselves to become a part of that person instead of showing individuality. This could be easily done without realizing that you have done it. Also, do you know that you can get so tied up in ministry that you actually start to put God's "people" before God? Yes, that can happen, and it actually happened to me. While I was praying to God, He brought to my attention that I was so involved in what He has called me to do that I was putting His people and their needs in front of Him and His needs, which was to guide me where He desires me to go. I was not getting my daily needs fed and supplied by God. I was running in front of Him, using His Word, yet not taking time to ask Him for clarity and direction.

Oh my, did I immediately repent and run right into His arms and just rest there for a long time. I immediately realized why I had been feeling down, drained, tired, frustrated, and unfulfilled, though happy and enjoying what I was doing for the ministry at the same time. Talk about confusion! I can't even explain or express my feelings, yet I remember them for the point of not ever doing that again. So, let's pray if you think this could be you.

Prayer: Father God, I repent for putting things, ministries, daily work, family, children, or anything else first in my life. I ask Your forgiveness and ask You to show me the way back to You that You may get all the glory, praise, and honor out of my life and all that I do, in Jesus' name, Amen!

Now get up, wipe your eyes, refocus on Jesus, and enjoy your life of abundance that Jesus came that we might have.

"The thief does not come except to steal, and to kill, and to destroy. I have come that they may have life, and that they may have it more abundantly" (John 10:10, NKJV).

Single by Widowhood

If you find yourself here, let's pray right now before even reading this.

Prayer: Father God, in Jesus' name, please heal my broken heart, emotions, hurt, pain, loneliness, anger, and any other feeling that I might have right now. I need to get a better understanding, and I need godly wisdom to receive the information I am getting ready to read in this book. Help me to do just that, in Jesus' name.

Talk to God from your deep inner being and share with Him how you really feel about losing your loved one. If you're angry, tell God. If you are hurting, tell God. If you're confused, tell God, but please be real because He knows how you feel anyway. Acts 15:8 tells us that God knows our hearts and thoughts. Don't try to put on a mask for God the way many put on a mask for church, work, and a lot of other functions. It's time we get real with God so that we can get real with ourselves and receive our healing.

Until you take off your old clothes, you cannot put new ones on, because you will look good on the outside, but once someone gets close to you, they will smell those dirty clothes you're still wearing underneath your new or clean ones. Matthew 9:12 tells us that you cannot put new wine in old wine skins; otherwise, they will burst. So, take time right now and ask God for help. Ask Jesus to touch you and heal you inside out. Ask for help because the Word of God tells us in Matthew 7:7 to "ask." Therefore, ask

God for help. He is the only one who knows how you feel and can heal your broken heart.

The loss of a loved one is something that can break you inside out. On October 29, 2015, I lost my ex-husband Jerry. Jerry and I were married for thirteen years and have known each other for almost twenty years. Jerry passed away very fast. It all happened so quickly that it still seems like a dream. Though we allowed the devil to come in and destroy our thirteen-year marriage (which also happened quickly), one thing I refused to allow the devil to do was to take away or destroy our "friendship." I fought for it and was victorious in Jesus' name. We remained good friends until the day he passed away. On that day, I realized that my heart did not know how to mourn an ex-husband. My heart only knew how to mourn and miss a loved one.

A loved one is just that, "a loved one," and that should never change, no matter what happens within a marriage or relationship. Divorce or anything else should never change your "unconditional love" for each other as believers in Jesus Christ. God's love is unconditional, and if we are confessing Jesus as our Lord and Savior, then our love should be unconditional, just as Christ's love is. I am so glad that I was obedient to the Word of God that says we should love one another as Christ has loved us. Make sure your love is "unconditional." I did, and I have no regrets after Jerry passed away. I dedicate this page to Jerry Grace. Rest in peace, Jerry. You will be missed by all that had an opportunity to meet you. Until the day we meet again in heaven.

Love,
Your friend, Penny.

Attitudes

One of Webster's definitions of "attitude" is "a settled way of thinking or feeling about someone or something, typically one that is reflected in a person's behavior."

However, we as believers should not judge a person by their outward behavior but find out; ask God what's at the root of how a person is acting. When you do this, you may find that a person is acting or behaving in an unpleasant way due to some deep down past or present hurt. Nothing to do with you, but what they are feeling/hurting from or going through. Ask God how to pray for that person or ask that person directly, "Is there anything that I can pray for you?" Even if their response is no, at least you have extended a hand instead of adding more hurt to their already deep-rooted pain. If you want to add something to someone's life, always make sure it's love and not hurt or hate!

Your attitude is something that always needs to be checked. Your attitude can determine your altitude because how you act and treat people can determine how far you will go in life and in the Lord. The wrong type of attitude expressed will cause you to draw certain types of people in and around you. If you have a don't-bother-me attitude, then you will get just that: no one will approach you or desire to spend time with you. If you have an "I'll-take-anything" attitude, then you will draw "anything" type of people into your life. Make sure that your attitude is that of gratitude toward God for all He has done and continues to do for you. You should be thankful for the small things so that you'll be blessed with greater things in life, as God sees how He can trust you to be "thankful" for everything.

It's not the size of the blessing, but the thought God was thinking about us when we were not thinking of Him. Sometimes, just like Martha, we are too busy to sit at the feet of Jesus and just love on Him and listen to what He has to say to us. God is talking, but His people are not listening and being obedient. Anytime you want to hear God speak, just sit down and read your Bible. He speaks clearly to us about everything in life, from Genesis to Revelation.

One day God told me to write down the word "busy," then He gave me the following: Jesus was never "BUSY" (Buried Under Satan's Yoke). Jesus was always about His Father's business. Therefore, I love how Jesus moved and responded to the crowds, His disciples, and the woman in Luke 8:40–48: Jesus stopped and allowed the woman with the blood issue, who touched Him and received immediate healing from her hemorrhaging to tell her story. Yes, Jesus took time, even though he was on His way to the house of a local leader of the synagogue because he had already come and fell at Jesus' feet pleading with Jesus to come home with Him because his only daughter who was twelve years old was dying. But Jesus stopped, took time for the woman with the issue of blood to tell Him her story. Now, people, you know, when most women and some men tell a story, we go from the beginning to the end, Amen! But Jesus stopped and allowed her to tell Him her story. That's definitely not busy but being about His Father's business and cares. Now, everyone will get to read and hear about this woman, her story, and her immediate healing because Jesus was not too busy to stop! This woman's story is in the Bible for all to read and experience her healing too. Yes, her faith and story have allowed her to be in the Holy Bible forever.

Attitudes (An Attitude of Gratitude)

Jesus took time even though someone already had a need and an emergency set up for Him, that did not stop Jesus from being about His Father's business. Amen! How many times do we pass by someone requiring a miracle from God and just keep on going to what we have set on our personal agenda? It really makes you think, huh. Let's be like Jesus and stay open-minded to what God's agenda is for us versus our own planned agenda, for the leader's daughter was restored back to life. Both the woman and the man received their blessing of total restoration that day. Read the entire story/experience below and decide right now to be like Jesus!

Jesus Heals a Bleeding Woman and Restores a Girl to Life

> Now when Jesus returned, a crowd welcomed him, for they were all expecting him. Then a man named Jairus, a synagogue leader, came and fell at Jesus' feet, pleading with him to come to his house because his only daughter, a girl of about twelve, was dying.
>
> As Jesus was on his way, the crowds almost crushed him. And a woman was there who had been subject to bleeding for twelve years, but no one could heal her. She came up behind him and touched the edge of his cloak, and immediately her bleeding stopped.
>
> 'Who touched me?' Jesus asked.
>
> When they all denied it, Peter said, 'Master, the people are crowding and pressing against you.'

But Jesus said, 'Someone touched me; I know that power has gone out from me.'

Then the woman, seeing that she could not go unnoticed, came trembling and fell at his feet. In the presence of all the people, she told why she had touched him and how she had been instantly healed. Then he said to her, 'Daughter, your faith has healed you. Go in peace.'

While Jesus was still speaking, someone came from the house of Jairus, the synagogue leader. 'Your daughter is dead,' he said. 'Don't bother the teacher anymore.'

Hearing this, Jesus said to Jairus, 'Don't be afraid; just believe, and she will be healed.'

When he arrived at the house of Jairus, he did not let anyone go in with him except Peter, John and James, and the child's father and mother. Meanwhile, all the people were wailing and mourning for her. 'Stop wailing,' Jesus said. 'She is not dead but asleep.'

They laughed at him, knowing that she was dead. But he took her by the hand and said, 'My child, get up!' Her spirit returned, and at once she stood up.

Then Jesus told them to give her something to eat.

Luke 8:40–55 (NIV)

Mary: Attitude of Faith and Acceptance

Mary knew that she would be stoned to death if found with a child out of wedlock. However, her answer to God's angel Gabriel was, "Behold the maidservant of the Lord! Let it be to me according to your word" (Luke 1:38, NKJV).

This is the type of attitude and faith God is asking us to have. Do you have it? Do you trust God, no matter what others will say or how others will treat you? These are two good questions that you need to ponder during your walk in Christ.

A Jezebel Attitude

You don't have to be a female to act like Jezebel. Jezebel is a type of "spirit" that has no respect for person, race, creed, color, or age. Jezebel, in the Bible, attacked the prophets of God. She hated authority and wanted what she wanted, how she wanted it, when she wanted it, at whatever cost, even a life. She was willing to kill more than one time to get what she wanted. Her husband had no control of her and used her to get what he wanted at one point as well. The flesh can never be satisfied. Neither can greed. The more you have, the more you want. The more you want, the more you are willing to do what you have to do to get what you want—simple things like becoming a workaholic, using people, telling on others to get them fired so that you can be moved into their job. The higher you get, the more power you believe you have (earthly).

This wrong thinking is just a trick of the devil to blind you and is not true, for there is a God who is and always will be higher than all of us. So, no matter how high you get, please be aware that you will always have to look up to God. It does not matter what you believe, think, justify, or not believe; you cannot change God. God is God, and no one will ever be able to do anything about that! Well, you may want to know if the devil/Satan is real. Yes, he is, but as followers of Jesus, we have authority over all of the devil's power. You just have to belong to Jesus to receive your authority (Luke 10:17–20). So change your attitude, and your life will change. Jesus is and has the answer to all of your problems. He is the "problem solver." Just trust Him!

Single After a Divorce

Now, who stands at an altar getting married and thinks about getting a divorce? That's right, no one does. Nor does any little girl or boy say, "I want to grow up and be divorced." It's just something that sometimes happens in life that will take you off track and into depression if you are not willing to redirect your mind and thoughts and allow God to heal your broken heart.

A divorce can be much like "death." It can be much like losing a loved one, with the exception of being even worse because you can see that loved one, and sometimes even with another woman/man, yet you must realize that you cannot be with him or her in the loving way you used to. Your mind can play so many games with your feelings and cause your heart to be broken. A divorce can stir up emotions that you have never experienced before, even anger to the point that you are willing to scream, fight, and kill the very same person with whom you stood in front of many people and confessed your love for life. Wow, how can that happen? Yes, it can happen quicker and easier than you can imagine.

Divorce touched a part in me that I didn't even realize existed. It felt as though something had been stolen from me while my back was turned and that by the time I turned around, everything was gone. I was left standing in the middle of the road, just wondering if and when I was going to get hit by an emotional car or a truck. It didn't matter because I could be taken out by either one. It wasn't about the size of the thing that hit me; it was just the fact that my entire being had been weakened by this "separation/divorce" thing. How could I get back on track and feel whole again?

Only God can put you back together again and create in you a desire to want to be made "whole," single, and satisfied. That's what God did for me. Yes, I am a living witness that God is real, and He will put you back together again. I have never been happier in my life. I never knew that my life would start at the age of almost sixty. You, too, can feel what I am feeling right now—"true happiness" (single and satisfied). Satisfied in who God created to be; loving unconditionally. Try and trust God. He will *never* fail you. But you have to want His help.

God will not touch our "free will" that He has given us; we always have a choice—God's way or our way are the alternatives. Many choose their way or the devil's way. Oh, yes, the devil does have his will for our life as well, but Jesus says in John 10:10 (NKJV), "The thief does not come except to steal, and to kill, and to destroy. I have come that they may have life, and that they may have *it* more abundantly."

If you don't think that Satan can influence God's people and get them to do what he wants them to do versus what God tells them to do, then take a break right now and read about the "fall of man" in the Holy Bible (Genesis, chapter 3).

Single After a Divorce

So now that you are back from your verification break, let's pray this prayer at the bottom of this page if you are divorced, and ask God to heal your heart, mind, thoughts, emotions, etc. It doesn't matter how you got to where you are; nothing is too hard or impossible for God to bring you back to Him and His unconditional love.

Prayer: Jesus, right now I feel so broken, hurt, unloved, rejected, and lonely, and I need You. Jesus, sometimes I even feel angry, possibly angry at You because I thought that You could have intervened and stopped my spouse from doing what he/she did. I thought that You could have even intervened and stopped me from doing what I did, but now I have come to the right understanding that You will not touch our free will, and it was not You or Your fault that my marriage/relationship was destroyed. I now realize that it was the devil that made us think that the grass was greener on the other side and that if we just leaped over and took a look at the other side, it wouldn't hurt anything. Well, Lord, here I am, and I give my total heart to You and ask You to heal my broken heart. I need You more than ever. My life I give to You and ask You to take it and change it to be what You desire me to be so that You will get the glory out of my life. Jesus, please go down deep; heal the hidden hurt and anger so that I may be single and satisfied in You and that You will get the glory out of this too, in Jesus' name, Amen!

Is Separation the Same as Divorce?

Separation is somewhat the same as divorce because it's the first step before a divorce. However, separation leaves great hope and the possibility of reconciliation. Nevertheless, the pain is the same because your life changes and someone is missing out on it. It's the step that brings the reality of what's happening in your life, in your marriage, and in your family. It's the step where you will start your "is this really happening" thoughts. It's the step where you will feel somewhat relieved sometimes, but then again lost and hurt at the same time. Your feelings are bouncing around back and forth like a basketball, or somewhat like a basketball game where everyone is sitting on the sidelines watching, spectating, and talking, yet no one knows who is going to win the game.

The point here is that life is more than a game; it never was and never will be. It's people, individuals, real-life changes, and no one knows but God what the outcome is going to be. Sometimes it could be reconciliation, divorce, death, or even watching the one you loved and thought would be in your life until the very end, the one you thought that you would grow old with, marry someone else. You will experience pain, hurt, anger, and frustration sometimes, but you must understand and know that there is *someone* who can heal your pain and deliver you out of all the hurt that you are experiencing. His name is Jesus, and all you have to do is acknowledge Him and ask Him to come into your heart and heal your brokenness.

He died for you, whether you believe it or not. He came and died for you that you may have eternal life with God. He purchased you back with His own blood as a final sacrifice so that Satan would lose his hold and control over you. You now can make a choice in whom you will serve, God or the devil. It's your choice.

In John 3:16–21, Jesus affirms,

> 'For God so loved the world that He gave His only begotten Son, that whoever believes in Him should not perish but have everlasting life. For God did not send His Son into the world to condemn the world, but that the world through Him might be saved. He who believes in Him is not condemned; but he who does not believe is condemned already, because he has not believed in the name of the only begotten Son of God. And this is the condemnation, that the light has come into the world, and men loved darkness rather than light, because their deeds were evil. For everyone practicing evil hates the light and does not come to the light, lest his deeds should be exposed. But he who does the truth comes to the light, that his deeds may be clearly seen, that they have been done in God.'
>
> John 3:16–21 (NKJV)

I believe we are missing the full impact and understanding of the Word of God when people only read or post billboards with just John 3:16 on them because more needs to be read. We need to get the full understanding of what God did, why God did it, and what we must do to have what God says we will have. God's love is unconditional, but God's Word is conditional. If we do what He tells us to do, then we will have what He says we will have, but if we don't do what God tells us to do, then we will not have what God says we will have. It's that clear and simple and does not need any justification from anyone. When God speaks, that's it!

Am I There Yet?
(Different Types of Love)

Divine Love, Romantic Love, Brotherly Love, Family Love
There are four types of love in the Bible. Which one/ones are you feeling and walking in right now?
1. Agape (the unconditional love of God);
2. Eros (romantic love);
3. Phileo (friendship love); and
4. Storge (love found especially between family members).

You cannot be whole when walking in "conditional" love. Conditional love is shown when everything is going well. It's contingent upon the circumstance and conditions as long as they are good. However, when something or anything bad/negative happens, especially if it hurts you, it's over, or your entire relationship changes. You are quick to shut down or give up. You just cannot seem to feel for that person as you used to. No matter what you try to do to get back to how you felt about him or her before he or she hurt you, you just can't seem to do it. So let the Lord help you.

If you're not walking in an Agape type of love (loving unconditionally), then you are not whole and will never learn to live a single, happy life until your heart is healed from all past hurt and pain. How do you know if you are still living from a place of past hurt and pain? If you are experiencing one or more of the following feelings when around people or when you are alone:

- your heart feels funny (flutters) when you see two people holding hands and showing deep affection toward each other;
- you feel you always have to defend yourself;
- your relationships or friendships never last long or as long as they used to;
- you don't want to get close to anyone or allow anyone to get close to you. You become distant and unconnected;
- you no longer believe that true love exists on earth;
- you become selfish and self-centered, wanting everything your way;
- you want to have your way, no matter whom you hurt or how you hurt the person, even and especially family members and your own children; and
- everything starts to annoy you and make you uncomfortable. You have no peace.

What's Love Got to Do with It?

Love has everything to do with it—it is your life, your relationships in life, your family, your mere being here on earth. If you want to be single and satisfied, you must first learn to love and forgive "yourself." Don't hold anything against you for making or not making the right decisions in life. You can always start over from where you are and move forward in life. Your past is just that, your past, and if you continue to think and dwell on your past, you will never have a "future." Yesterday is gone, and you can never recover it, so find out what is ahead because you know what was behind.

You must also forgive yourself. After forgiving yourself, you must now forgive everyone else as well. Make no excuses; forgive them. Stop giving them the power over you, which is stopping you from moving on in life. You will never be able to be single and satisfied unless you learn to "forgive." Forgiveness is a freedom that we all need within ourselves. We need it within our inner being. Stop allowing your inner "me" to be your "enemy." The most important reason that we should forgive is given by Jesus in Matthew 6:15 (NIV). Jesus admonishes, "But if you do not forgive others their sins, your Father will not forgive your sins."

I want you to stop right now, write down three things that you like about yourself, one reason why you love yourself, and one person you need to forgive.

One month from now, I want you to come back and read them again.

1.

2.

3.

Well, here is the one thing I like and celebrate daily about me that I would like to share with you:

1. God created me in His image. He loves me unconditionally, and nobody or nothing can change that!

Prayer: Father God, in the name of Jesus, I desire to forgive; please teach me to forgive so that I can forgive myself and learn how to forgive others as well. Lord, show me "Your ways" that I may give unconditional love to everyone, in Jesus' name, Amen!

I like what the Psalmist says in Psalm 25:4–5 (NIV): "Show me your ways, Lord, teach me your paths. Guide me in your truth and teach me, for you are God my Savior, and my hope is in you all day long."

How I Learned to Love Again after a Divorce

One day, while sitting and watching TV with my grandson, for no reason and without realizing what I was doing, I leaned over, pulled him closer to me, and kissed him on the back of his head. Without realizing what I had done, I felt a warm feeling inside of me that I had never felt before. I asked, "God, is this the way You love me?" God spoke to my heart and said, "No, My love for you is even greater."

My entire life changed at that very moment, and I made a conscious decision that I would love with an unconditional love. No matter what people do to me, I will not allow anything to take away or alter this unconditional love from God that I am feeling right now.

God used my grandson to show me how to love again. It's not that I didn't love or was not showing love to God's people, but the unconditional love of God that I received from the Holy Spirit upon accepting Jesus as Lord and Savior of my life had lost its true meaning and feeling within the deep and inner part of my being. I allowed circumstances and situations, the cares of this world, to take away and alter my ability to love, which God had given to me. Now I know why Jesus says not to let the cares of this world weigh you down: "Be careful, or your hearts will be weighed down with carousing, drunkenness and the anxieties of life, and that day will close on you suddenly like a trap" (Luke 21:34, NIV).

I have always felt that the unconditional love residing with me has always been a "gift" from God. As far as I can remember back (age of two), I was never able to hate or dislike someone because of what he or she did to me. Even to this day, no matter what anyone does to me, I can always forgive them from my heart and love them from my heart. Now, this does not mean that I keep him or her in my life or continue to spend time with him or her; it just means that I know how to move on and love on.

Sometimes people are put in your life for a short time, long time, or a "meantime," but like Jesus, we must keep going until we fulfill our God-given purpose and destiny. Jesus knew that His purpose on earth was to die for us and redeem us back from Satan. We, too, must understand that our purpose on earth is to fulfill our God-given purpose/destiny here, then die a physical death so that we, too, just like Jesus, can return to our Father and spend eternity with Him.

I will not let the cares and causes of this life deter me from my God-given destiny, and I hope that right now, while you are reading this book, you will come on one accord with me. Why don't you, right now, at this point, accept Jesus as your Lord and Savior by repeating the following prayer: Jesus, I'm tired of living this life that I am living. Please come into my life right now, come into my heart, change me, and show me how to live the life that You died for me to have so that I can have eternal life with God. I renounce Satan and all his evil and sinful ways right now. I ask You to forgive me, accept me the way I am right now, and then change me into what You desire me to be. Jesus, I believe that You died for me and now live, sitting on the right hand of God, interceding for me. Take me, Jesus, right now. I give myself and my life to You and ask You to baptize me with the Holy Spirit. Thank you, Jesus, Amen.

How I Learned to Love Again after a Divorce

Now, just move on, and the Spirit of God will lead and guide you daily on what to do and how to do it. Call a prayer line, go to a local church, and let a leader know that you just asked Jesus to come into your heart and that you want someone to pray with you. Don't be afraid; just enjoy your new life in Jesus. I have been enjoying my new life for many years and plan to enjoy it until it's my time to cross over to the other side. God bless you for taking time to read this book, but most of all, for accepting Jesus as Lord and Savior of your life.

Second Corinthians 5:17 says that you are a new creature now; all things are new and old things are passed away.

> He died for everyone so that those who receive his new life will no longer live for themselves. Instead, they will live for Christ, who died and was raised for them. So we have stopped evaluating others from a human point of view. At one time we thought of Christ merely from a human point of view. How differently we know him now! This means that anyone who belongs to Christ has become a new person. The old life is gone; a new life has begun! And all of this is a gift from God, who brought us back to himself through Christ. And God has given us this task of reconciling people to him. For God was in Christ, reconciling the world to himself, no longer counting

people's sins against them. And he gave us this wonderful message of reconciliation.

                        2 Corinthians 5:15–19 (KJV)

Single and Waiting for a Husband

It's all in how you wait and what you're doing while waiting!

"Wait, I say on the Lord!" "Waiting" means that you are in a place where you want to be married yet still single. You are still waiting totally on God and trusting God to prepare you and present you to that special earthly man of God. Well, while you are waiting, you should be asking God to help you be the wife that the man is praying for. It's a wonderful time to work on yourself and the goals you have set for yourself in life through prayer. A lot of women have the definition of their choice for a husband totally wrong. God knows who and what's best for you, so trust Him to choose the right man for you. After all, God created man, and only God knows what's inside man. Remember, we look on the outside, but God sees the inside:

> But the Lord said to Samuel, 'Do not consider his appearance or his height, for I have rejected him. The Lord does not look at the things people look at. People look at the outward appearance, but the Lord looks at the heart.'
>
> 1 Samuel 16:7 (NIV).

I'm not telling you to turn your nose up at anyone, nor am I saying that any man is less than you, but the one that you have been praying for and the one who God has chosen to give you to will fit in your prayer request and be even greater than what you asked God for.

Now, we do have women who just pray for a "husband." However, we do have women who pray for God's "perfect will" regarding their chosen spouses. After many falls due to my own choices, not God's, finally, I have decided to pray for God's "perfect will" versus God's "permissive will," which mean I may have to wait longer, but it will be worth my wait when God's plan comes together. Therefore, in the meantime, while I am waiting, I choose to do the work of the Lord and pour out all of myself into helping others. Right now, I am moving in the ministry that God has entrusted me with, Reaching Millions Ministries (ReachingMillionsMinistries.com), and also doing all I can to assist pastors and leaders, as well as all of God's servants and people in any and every area they are in need of my assistance and gifts. I plan to utilize every free moment I have, doing whatever I can to be a blessing to others, including writing other books that I pray will bless God's people all over the world. Women, while you are waiting, and in your meantime, what do you plan to do? Pray about it right now! But choose to wait on the Lord and let Him present you to the man, just like He did with Rebecca to Isaac. Do not try to place yourself in front of the man by just jumping in front of any man. Remember, when you jump in front of something, you can get hit (your heart hurt) because they may not be expecting it, and it does not feel good. But if you wait on the Lord and Him present you to the man, then you will feel like a jewel and a chosen one, an answer to His prayer. I desire to be an answer to my husband's prayer, not his unexpected surprise. I never pray to God for a husband; I pray and ask God to show me how to be a wife. God already has the husband chosen for me. I desire to be the queen for my king, so together we can both serve the King of all Kings, Jesus Christ!

Single and Waiting for a Wife

Men, I have been waiting for a very long time to talk to you about your choices in marriage. Just like women, you, too, sometimes choose to marry someone you know is not good for you or really in love with you. You feel that you can change her, rescue her, or get her to love you later on after marrying her. You even try buying her material things to please her so she will marry and love you always. Men, this is not true. If she does not cook and tells you that before you get married, why do you think that you are going to marry her and she will magically turn into a "cook"? Believe her when she tells you that she is:

- not a cook, nor going to cook;
- a messy person and does not like cleaning;
- not fond of nor want to have children; and
- a party girl, which will turn into a partying selfish woman (remember that a selfish child equals a selfish adult if not redirected/taught otherwise).

Ask God, "Is this the right woman that He has chosen for you?" Then, watch how she walks out of her relationship with the Lord. If she does not have a committed, respectful relationship to and with Jesus, then she will not be in a committed respectful relationship with you. Remember, God looks at the heart.

God will give you a wife according to where you are going, not where you are now. A wife who is willing and able to go and grow with you, not trying to stop you from growing. The wife is presented to you like Rebecca was to Isaac. He was not looking for a wife; his wife was presented to him according to where God was sending him. The question should be, "Can she handle where you are going, not just where you are right now?"

Men, wait, I say on the Lord. The Lord will seek out and find you a wife that will join you in your devotion to God because He sees her heart. Her outside will change several times throughout life, but if her heart belongs to the Lord, then that's what matters.

Why don't you stop right here and take time to read about Isaac and Rebecca in Genesis 24:1–67. Make sure you take mental and physical notes for yourself. Also, write down a few things that you plan on doing while waiting on the Lord. Work on yourself and increase your faith and devotion to God during this time. Yes, enjoy your S.A.S. season.

---------------Welcome back from your reading break---------------

So now that you're back, I hope you enjoyed reading about Isaac and Rebecca, and I pray that you are encouraged to wait on the Lord. Don't get anxious, but be of good courage; He knows the desires of your heart. Remember that a "no" is not rejection; it's protection. Therefore, seek God for a wife and allow Him to protect your heart, ministry, and future by waiting on His choice for you, not yours.

Feeling Single and Alone after the Death of a Child (A Parent's Devastation)

Wow, a parent would never imagine being at this stage in their life. It sounds so unreal for a parent to have to bury their child. This is a life-changing hurt/tragedy, no matter how they leave this earth. No one could tell you not to cry or grieve because this is needed to heal your inner you, the part that has developed a relationship with this child from birth and has been devasted. You carried this child in your womb and in your heart even before the very beginning. Whether it's by natural or by adoption, it doesn't matter. You have carried that child in your mind, thoughts, and heart, even before they arrived. The arrival doesn't make the child yours; the heart does. Try to realize that your life is not over; you still have loved ones here on earth that need you, love you, and want to help you. You are not alone! Don't hurt the ones here that are trying to help you because of your heart feeling totally crushed and destroyed. Take time to grieve in your own way, but don't forget that you are not alone in your devastation. Cry out to God for help and healing, for He is the *only* One who truly knows how you feel. He is God, and He knows all. He can and will heal your brokenness. For God is:

Omnipotent—God is all-powerful. He spoke all things into being, and all things—every cell, every breath, every thought—are sustained by Him. Nothing is too difficult for Him (Jeremiah 32:17–18; Jeremiah 32:26–27).

Omniscient—God is all-knowing. God's knowledge encompasses every possible thing that exists, has ever existed, or will ever exist. Nothing is a mystery to Him. All things are open and laid bare to the eyes of Him with whom we have to give account (Hebrews 4:13).

Omnipresent—God is everywhere, in and around everything, close to everyone (Psalm 139:7–12).

So please be encouraged and know that God is right there with you; He sees your every tear. God is watching and helping you go through all your grief and pain.

Feeling Single and Alone after the Death of a Child (A Parent's Devastation)

I watched two of my siblings go through several different stages of grief after the passing of their child, but one thing I witnessed was God being there and carrying them through every second of their grief. You must trust God and ask God for help. Also, seek professional counseling for your grief if needed. Seek out someone with the same beliefs that you have and have a personal relationship with Jesus also. You're in a very vulnerable stage of your life, and you do not want the enemy to use this time to come in and destroy all that God has done in you and your life. Don't ever give up; just give in to Jesus and watch Him walk in and with you every second of your life. My two sisters and their families are still to this day, trusting and totally depending on the Lord to bring them through each day, and yes, He is doing that above and beyond their expectations and mine too. Each one is moving forward in life knowing that they will get to reunite with their child/loved ones on the other side.

Prayer: Father God, you promised me that You would never leave me or forsake me; You promised me that You will be with me until the end of time. Father, right now, I feel like it's the end of my time because my heart is so broken and crushed from this loss in my life. I turn to You, for Jesus says in Luke 4:18 (KJV), "I was sent to heal the brokenhearted." My heart needs healing right now, Father, and I ask You to heal my broken heart, give me Your strength every second of my life, for I cannot, and I do not want to go through life feeling crushed/broken like this when Jesus says in John 10:10 (KJV), "I am come that they might have life, and that they might have it more abundantly." Heal me in every area that I am hurting Father, that I may have an abundant life and not just exist, day by day here on earth, in Jesus' name I ask and pray, Amen.

A few more encouraging scriptures:

> "He heals the brokenhearted and binds up their wounds" (Psalm 147:3, NIV).

> "The LORD is close to the brokenhearted and saves those who are crushed in spirit" (Psalm 34:18, NIV).

> "Cast all your anxiety on him because he cares for you" (1 Peter 5:7, NIV).

I Am Born Again/a Believer, Now What?

Congratulations on your newborn-again life in Christ. Now that you have accepted Jesus as your personal Lord and Savior, you don't want to stop there. Your next step is to get to know Jesus so that you can follow Him daily. You want to have a personal relationship with Jesus. Just as when you meet someone you like for the first time, you want to get to know the person better, so you try to spend time, quality time, together. Likewise, do the same with Jesus. Spend time reading about Him and what He did while He walked the earth. Find out how He lived here on earth, where He is now and how you can get to know Him better. Desire a close personal relationship with Jesus, just not a quick meet and greet session.

Jesus wants to have a close relationship with us. Jesus died for us. He gave His life so that we may be restored back to God and spend eternity with God. Jesus, while He was praying to God in John 17:3 (NKJV), prays, "And this is eternal life, that they may know You, the only true God, and Jesus Christ whom You have sent." Jesus also says, "If anyone desires to come after Me, let him deny himself, and take up his cross daily, and follow Me" (Luke 9:23, NKJV).

This new life that you have accepted in Christ is a daily walk. You don't stop walking in it until you go to spend eternity with God. Every day should be a day that you live for God, and that will bring you closer to spending eternity with Him. That's why we must walk in obedience to God, as we are led and guided by the Holy Spirit (God's Spirit). The Holy Spirit is our guide and our leader. He will always remind us what the Word of God tells us to do. The Holy Spirit will always lead and guide us according to what He hears God telling us to do and where He is telling us to go. That's why it is imperative that you also learn about the Holy Spirit (read Acts). There is so much to learn and enjoy as you grow in your new walk in Christ. What a wonderful experience you are about to have as you walk in your new life in Christ. You must now allow Jesus to be Lord over *everything* you are and *everything* you have. Give it all to Jesus. Why don't you start now by praying the prayer below?

"Jesus, now that I am yours, I desire to align the desires of my heart up with the desires of Your heart. Jesus, I give You my heart and ask You to put Your desires in my heart." (Pray Psalm 37 along with this prayer.) I also ask to be filed with the Holy Spirit with the evidence of speaking in tongues.

It's that simple—very profound and effective, yet simple to understand and pray. Now just surrender your all to the Lord and enjoy your daily walk in Christ, knowing that no matter what happens, He is with you. Then don't stop here; continue to add faith to your new life daily:

> For this very reason, make every effort to add to your faith goodness; and to goodness, knowledge; and to knowledge, self-control; and to self-control, perseverance; and to perseverance, godliness; and to godliness, mutual affection; and to mutual affection, love. For if you possess these qualities in increasing measure, they will keep you from being ineffective and unproductive in your knowledge of our Lord Jesus Christ.
>
> 2 Peter 1:5–8 (NIV)

A Queen-Vashti Attitude?

"Husband, I'm too busy to come or go right now."

Vashti was a queen in the Book of Esther. As you see, I said, "was a queen."

I read in the Book of Esther about how King Xerxes held a banquet celebration and that Queen Vashti decided to throw a ball for the wives of the kings as well. However, after he was pretty drunk, King Xerxes sent for Queen Vashti to show her off, but Queen Vashti was too busy entertaining with her own banquet guests (Esther 1:9). Therefore, Queen Vashti refused to obey the king and come (Esther 1:12).

Now let's just stop right here and reflect on our lives before cutting Queen Vashti up and down the middle. How many times have we been called by someone in higher leadership than ourselves or even our husbands, and we decided that we were not going to go? We even tell them that we are not going to go with them, or even worse than that, send them by themselves to some affair or function that we do not want to attend. I thought that would bring you back to yourself. So, now that you're back, let's continue with Queen Vashti's story and attitude.

King Xerxes was very angry, distraught, and embarrassed in front of all the other kings, leaders, slaves, etc., so of course, King Xerxes had to dethrone Queen Vashti to show his kingship and authority. She lost her position as queen, was never allowed to go before the king again, and was replaced by a very humble and appreciative damsel, now Queen Esther.

Remember: when you don't want to go, there will always be another woman/man who is willing to go in your stead. So, a single and satisfied mind would be willing to make an unselfish move and take a walk, talk, time to share, and be with others when she/he would rather be alone.

Some may say that maybe Queen Vashti did not want King Xerxes to show her off as a piece of merchandise, but we must remember she knew what being queen meant before she became queen. We cannot take or enjoy the wonderful rewards of our position and not want to deal with the not-so-wonderful ones. So, if you decide to take a position or office, be willing to walk all the way through to the end, that God may get the glory. Don't get to your divine destiny and turn it into a disaster. God will open doors for you to get there, but He will not force you to stay. Therefore, ask yourself the following question:

Are you too BUSY (Buried Under Satan's Yoke) because of:

church boards	committees	hospitality committees
deacon board	usher board	pastor's aide
mother board	praise team/choir	
your job/work		

Just This, That and All the Rest

Where are your priorities? Who comes first in your life? How do you react when your spouse asks you to do something?

A "Mary Attitude"

Your attitude will define your ultimate latitude. If you keep a positive attitude, then you will see things differently. For instance, your car breaks down. Instead of getting angry and acting out, you could just think, *Wow! I am so glad that I have AAA, that my best friend is a mechanic*, or just any positive thought you can release rather than getting mad about an ordinary thing that is likely to happen to anyone. Your car is a vehicle, not a "god." Always stay positive, and you will learn how to make lemonade out of all the crushed lemons that come with everyday life experiences. Jesus says in John 16:33 (NKJV), "These things I have spoken to you, that in Me you may have peace. In the world you will have tribulation; but be of good cheer, I have overcome the world."

Those who confess to Jesus as their Lord and Savior must try to keep a positive outlook on life so that they can be able to help others who are in need of help coming out of a dark world into the marvelous light that Jesus is in us.

Mary was already espoused to be married to Joseph when she was impregnated by the Holy Spirit. What made Mary the chosen woman to carry the "only begotten son," our Holy God? Let's look at Mary's attitude when she was approached by an angel of God in Luke 1:38 (KJV): "And Mary said, 'Behold the handmaid of the Lord; be it unto me according to thy word.' And the angel departed from her."

Overcoming Times of Frustration

You may be saying, "I know that God is able. I have heard all the prophesies and testimonies. I have been prophesized to, but right now, I still feel frustrated. So how do I deal with bouts of frustration?" According to Webster's definition, the word "frustration" means: "The feeling of being upset or annoyed, especially because of inability to change or achieve something." Therefore, it may be that you are trying to do something in your own will versus the will and power of God? Why not just let go and let God step in and lead and guide you of what His plan is for you? At that very moment, you feel this frustration coming in you. You have tried your way, now try God's way, and watch a wonderful change and peace come into your heart when you give up and give in to the One who created you, and is able to turn your situation, circumstance, and entire life around.

While you are in between the doors of yesterday and tomorrow, it can be very frustrating at times. However, this is where you will find your strength while increasing your faith and belief in God and His Word. Increase who you are and what He has called you to be. You can't get fresh orange juice without squeezing some oranges. So don't let the devil cause you to not enjoy your "in-between" season. Remember that Ecclesiastes says, "There is a time and season..."

Each season brings a different type of bloom, fruit, and weather to your life. Without the rain in April, May flowers would not look so beautiful. It's not fun driving, walking, and trying to do things through the rainy month of April. In May, however, when the weather is just perfect, the flowers will bloom because the rain has fed the roots their needed water. You didn't understand the rain and what it would benefit during the month of April. You didn't understand that the soil needed the rainwater to feed it so that it could keep the seed moist and nourished. So when people are admiring the beautiful flowers in May, they forget about the rainy days that were not appreciated at that time in April. Likewise, we don't want to go through the cold, rainy days in our lives, which are needed and required to bring out the fruit in our lives after the rain is over. In order for us to see the rainbow, there has to be rain. So don't get angry or frustrated when rain comes into your life. Instead, ask God to cover you with His umbrella (that allows some rain to come through) and protect you as the rain falls to nourish what He has implanted within you that, in the time of bloom, everything He has implanted within you shall rise and bloom. Then others will be able to enjoy and get blessed from the rain in your life.

Also, in order to become fruit, a seed must be planted deep down in the dirt, covered, watered so that it will live again in a more beautiful form right here on earth. Bear in mind that whatever you plant, that's what you shall reap. What did you plant in your life that you are reaping now? Good seeds or evil seeds? For you shall reap what you have sowed when it's harvest time.

Prayer: Father God, in Jesus' name, I repent for any evil seeds that I have knowingly or unknowingly planted in my life and ask You, in Jesus' name, to reveal it to me. Then allow me to dig deep, uproot each nonproductive seed, and replant it in good and fertile soil that I may reap good rewards from them, all in Your time Father. I pray this prayer in the name of Jesus, Amen!

Who Can I Talk to, and How Can They Help Me?

Nothing is wrong with seeking professional help if you need it. However, if you are a believer in Jesus Christ, then you should seek a faith-like person who can better help you seek Jesus for deep revelation and assistance in your time of need. Why? It's very simple. First Corinthians 3:19 (KJV) says, "For the wisdom of this world is foolishness with God. For it is written, He taketh the wise in their own craftiness." So if you don't have Jesus as your Savior, then you don't have the Spirit of God in you; therefore, you cannot get a revelation/knowledge of what is really happening or should happen in your life or anyone else's life around you. You see things from the darkness that you are in.

God bought us out of darkness into the marvelous light, so don't expect people to understand you or be able to help you when they are still in the darkness. You can also go to the elders of your church or your pastor and ask for assistance. If they are not available to assist you at that time, then they will surely refer you to someone or have someone to pray for you and contact you in your time of need.

As a servant of the Most High God, I can say that the first thing I am is a servant, and therefore, I am honored to pray for and assist God's people when they are in a time of need. After all, many times have I been in the same situation (in need) of someone to pray for me or talk to me, and God never failed me.

However, sometimes you need to seek God for yourself because as you are seeking Him, then you are establishing and growing in your relationship with Him.

It is imperative that you have a relationship with the Lord because how can you get to know Him and desire to spend eternity with Him when you don't have a relationship with God? You get a relationship with God through His only begotten Son, Jesus. God is the only one who can fulfill your every need, even the deep-down ones that no one knows about, even you sometimes, and Jesus is the only way to God. "Jesus said to him, 'I am the way, the truth, and the life. No one comes to the Father except through Me'" (John 14:6, NKJV).

Married but Single

Every time you tell someone that you are single, the person automatically assumes that you have never been married. However, you can be married and still be single. You can be single in your thought pattern—ways of not sharing or wanting to share with your spouse; single in regards to taking care of and doing things with/for your child(ren). As a "Mommy"/"Daddy," you could have a high-powered job, which leaves you "single" in a "married life."

Many may be now looking at the First Lady, wife of the President of the United States, and admiring her in numerous ways. However, if the real story were to be told, then everyone would know that every First Lady has to live a very solitary and circumspect life. She must give up her husband for a very long time in order to support and be there for him as he goes about carrying out his duties as President of the United States of America.

Sometimes, in a marriage, one spouse must walk in a "single" lifestyle in order for the other spouse to reach their family's set goal. Then, after the goal is accomplished, the entire family benefits, and that "single lifestyle" proves to be worth all the efforts put into it, for everyone is able to enjoy the fruit now.

It's very easy to look at someone else's life and admire this person for what you see her or him as or who you think she or he is because of her or his lifestyle. However, we must always remember that a worldwide figure, such as a United States President, was not born into the position or office in which they are now walking.

It took a lot to get the person there, and it will take even more to keep the person there. We should be thankful for who we are, and especially for who God has created us, to be made in His image, and as loving beings, we should love God with all our heart, soul, mind, and strength, and love one another as Christ loves us. Now, there are two ways that we should try "to walk" our love life out, and these two ways we should try to pattern our lives after. Jesus spoke to them below:

> 'Love the Lord your God with all your heart and with all your soul and with all your mind and with all your strength.' The second is this: 'Love your neighbor as yourself.' There is no commandment greater than these.
>
> Mark 12:30–31 (NIV)

> "A new commandment I give unto you, That ye love one another; as I have loved you, that ye also love one another" (John 13:34, KJV).

Without love, we do not have God in us, nor in our life. It's that simple for those who confess Jesus as their Lord and Savior (believers of Christ/Christians) because the Holy Bible tells us in 1 John 4:8 (NASB), "The one who does not love does not know God, because God is love."

Single and Pregnant

God created a woman with a womb so that she would be able to carry a child. No matter how a man may try to alter his body, the realization is this: God, the *only* Creator of *all* creations, created *only* a *woman* with a *womb*, not a man. Man carries the seed, not the woman, and *no one* will ever be able to alter this original creation fact that differentiates a man from a woman!

If you are single and pregnant, God's love for you has not changed. He still loves you just as much as He loves all His other creations unconditionally. The Word of God tells us in Romans 8:38 that nothing can separate us from the love of God. However, please don't get this mixed up with being separated from God because our sins can and will separate us from our Holy God. However, repentance brings salvation, and salvation brings restoration back to God. That's why Jesus came to restore and redeem us back to God through the shedding of His Blood as the final and ultimate sacrifice.

At this time in your life, you may feel alone, or it may seem that there is a void in your life. Please be encouraged by the Word of God in Matthew 28:20 (NIV), as Jesus says, "And surely I am with you always, to the very end of the age."

Jesus will never leave you nor forsake you. No matter who walks out on you at this time in your life, no matter who puts you out of his/her life or house, know that God is still with you even when you don't want Him to be. God is faithful and loving to all His creations even when His creation is not faithful or loving toward Him.

Now that you have found yourself in this position, it does not mean that your life is over; it's just altered, as another life is starting in nine months. Don't allow hate, frustration, confusion, rejection, or any other negative spirit to slip into your life. Don't contemplate abortion because you will have to live with that decision for the rest of your life. What seems right to do at this moment may not seem right next week or even next month. Therefore, try to find someone you can talk to that you trust. Then allow God to speak to you through this sought-out individual. Help is always a phone call, walk, talk away.

Prayer: Father God, first, I repent and ask Your forgiveness for my sins that got me here, in the name of Jesus. I realize that Your love has not changed for me; therefore, it shall be Your love, and Your grace and Your mercy and Your strength that I will need to move forward to take care of this child that I am carrying. Help me to not be too proud to ask for help for the ones that you direct me to. Help me to forgive myself and not dwell on the negatives of life. Help me to learn all that I need to learn to be a good mother and servant of Yours, Father. Help me to move past the embarrassment and finger-pointing that I may run into and help me to not return evil for evil but walk in Your love daily as I chose Your way over my way and especially the world's way. Father God, Your Word says in Isaiah 26:3 (KJV) that "Thou wilt keep *him* in perfect peace *whose* mind *is* stayed on *thee*: because he trusteth in thee." Father God, I need inner peace to go through this. I need the kind of peace that Jesus speaks of giving us in John 14:27 (NKJV), "Peace I leave with you, My peace I give to you; not as the world gives do I give to you. Let not your heart be troubled, neither let it be afraid." Father God, I thank You for hearing and answering my prayer, for I press through all the hurt, pain, and shame, and I pray this in Jesus' name, Amen!

Knowledge

Knowledge is the state of being aware of something. Knowledge can come in and from a lot of different ways or things that we have gone through, but true knowledge—which we need to take us through our earthly life and situations—is best when it comes from God. He knows all and can see into our future, as well as our daily walk here on earth.

I may know something, but even though I know about it doesn't mean I know how to conquer it. For instance, I may know how to drive, but to get behind the wheel and apply my knowledge is another ordeal and will not keep me from having an accident even when I become an experienced driver.

King Solomon was given great wisdom from God (1 Kings 3:1–12). However, even with his great wisdom received from God, King Solomon did not use knowledge with his wisdom when it came to women. King Solomon, just like his father, King David, had a weakness for women and did not know how to control it. Those who share this weakness must ask God for His strength in this area and others that you know you are weak in. First, ask God to show you as well as tell you where your weaknesses are. It could be in one area or in many areas of your life/within you. It could be deeply suppressed and have come from several generations before you. Once God shows it/them to you, ask Him to strengthen you and deliver you in those areas.

Wisdom

Wisdom is the natural ability to understand things that most other people cannot understand. Godly wisdom is the supernatural ability to understand things that most people cannot understand nor see how you came to see that deep within a person, people, or situations. God's wisdom supersedes that of humans. After all, God is the Creator of every living being and thing. God is the Creator of the universe. God is omniscient (knows all) and omnipresent (everywhere at the same time). God is God! No man/woman can explain Him or define Him. He is God, and that's it. Therefore, like King Solomon, we need to pray and ask Him to give us His wisdom so that we will be able to do and know everything in a higher and greater understanding than our human abilities can reach or do on their own.

God has an infinite (unlimited) mind. He is always awake. He never sleeps. We need our sleep and rest so that we can function on a daily basis, and if we don't get the proper amount of sleep/rest, then our bodies will not function correctly, and we are unable to think and process information properly. Wisdom is a must for all of God's people on earth. Even animals need rest and sleep. For instance, the bear goes into hibernation once a year. Who do you think gave the bears wisdom to rest/sleep yearly and calls them to sleep/rest? God. Who do you think put that thought/wisdom in their minds? Yes, it had to be God because animals, unlike humans, cannot read about what they need or should do to keep themselves healthy and living. So God even gives wisdom to the animals, too.

The Bible tells us in James 1:5 (NKJV), "If any of you lacks wisdom, let him ask of God, who gives to all liberally and without reproach, and it will be given to him."

Now, let's pray: Father God, in the name of Jesus, we come to You, asking You to search deep down within our innermost being and show us the area or areas that we are weak in and in need of Your strength. Then, Father, give us Your strength, wisdom, and knowledge, and build us up in those areas so that we may walk in Your strength and be healed and delivered from our weakness, in Jesus' name, Amen.

Wisdom and Knowledge Together

Wisdom (to know something) and knowledge (know how/when to apply wisdom) together can be empowering and very powerful. When you know something and know how to do it, then you are able to conquer certain things and even show or teach others how to do the same.

The Bible tells us that faith without work is dead. So you may have a very strong belief in or about something, but if you don't act upon it, then nothing is going to happen. You may know that you have an ability or gift to play the piano, but until you sit down at the piano and try to play something, you will never know if you can play or not.

Don't be afraid to step out in faith and do what God has called you to do. Seek God for all you need in life. Nothing is too small or impossible with God. After all, what's wrong with doing something even though you are afraid to do it? Just pray, and then do whatever God tells you to do. Just do it—not because it's a cliché from Nike, but because the Bible encourages me that "I can do all things through Christ which strengtheneth me" (Philippians 4:13, KJV). Therefore, let's pray.

Prayer: Lord, please give me Your wisdom to understand things and the knowledge to be able to apply Your wisdom in every area of my life and my family's life in everything we do, in Jesus' name, Amen.

Now, start listening carefully for the still, quiet voice of God as He leads and guides you by His Spirit (the Holy Spirit) daily. This needs to be done daily because our walk of salvation is a daily walk. We learn on a daily basis. Life is taking it one day at a time, not week-by-week, month-by-month, or year-by-year—just one day at a time.

Why Do I Need to Be Born Again (Saved)?

Man is a sinner, and sin has separated him from God!

You may think you are a good person but being good is not enough! Every man has sinned, and there is none that is righteous before God! "For there is not a just man upon earth, that doeth good, and sinneth not" (Ecclesiastes 7:20, KJV).

"For all have sinned, and come short of the glory of God" (Romans 3:23, KJV).

Jesus Christ is the only remedy for sin. He is and always will be the ultimate and final sacrifice. Without Him, we cannot be good enough to get into heaven, nor can our good works/deeds get us there.

There was no other way for God to erase the effect of sin except by blood. The shedding of Christ's blood indicated that the penalty for sin had been paid; a perfect, sinless life had been sacrificed for the lives of all who have sinned. "And almost all things are cleansed with blood, according to the Law, and without the shedding of blood there is no forgiveness" (Hebrews 9:22, NASB).

"For Christ also suffered once for sins, the just for the unjust, that He might bring us to God, being put to death in the flesh but made alive by the Spirit" (1 Peter 3:18, NKJV).

"Neither is there salvation in any other: for there is none other name under heaven given among men, whereby we must be saved" (Acts 4:12, KJV).

You must receive Jesus Christ as your Lord and Savior.

To be saved, a man/woman must confess that Jesus is Lord while acknowledging in his heart that Christ must have full rule over his life. This confession of Christ as Lord assumes that it is Christ who will work and fulfill His own righteousness within man, as man is unable to attain righteousness of his own accord.

Jesus calls this experience the "new birth." He told Nicodemus in John 3:3 (KJV), "Except a man be born again, he cannot see the kingdom of God."

Forgiveness/Unforgiveness

Forgiveness is for your good, not only for the person you can't forgive but for you. Unforgiveness builds inner anger and resentment toward the person/people who hurt you. Holding onto this type of inner anger and bitterness can cause you to become physically ill at one point in your life. Have you ever noticed that the person with whom you are so angry seems to keep moving forward and that you are still left behind "angry"? Now this anger is only adding to and building upon the way you feel. You don't have to have dinner and continue to visit or hang out with the person/people, but you do need to forgive them so that you can move forward with your life. Being single and satisfied will help you do this, as you are not concentrating on getting to know or understand anyone but yourself for a specific time period of your life. Learn how to be happy with how God created you (in His image). Then you can spend more time enjoying life and not being angry with life. Jesus says in Matthew 6:14–15 (KJV), "For if ye forgive men their trespasses, your heavenly Father will also forgive you: But if ye forgive not men their trespasses, neither will your Father forgive your trespasses." So, forgive and start enjoying life!

A Special Invitation

I invite you now to receive the Lord Jesus Christ as your personal Savior. The Holy Bible tells us in John 1:12 (KJV), "But as many as received him, to them gave he power to become the sons of God, even to them that believe on his name."

If you are serious about changing your life and really desire to be single and satisfied, you must first be saved (born again). So please pray this prayer from your heart and invite Jesus into your heart and into your life.

Pray: dear Lord Jesus, I realize that I am a sinner and have broken Your laws. I understand that my sin has separated me from God. I repent, and I ask You to forgive me. Jesus, I accept the fact that You died for me, were resurrected, and are alive today and hear my prayers. I now open my heart and invite Jesus to come into my heart and become my Lord and Savior. I give Jesus control and ask that He would rule and reign in my heart so that His perfect will would come to pass in my life. I renounce Satan and his ways and ask You, Jesus, to fill me with the Holy Spirit. Amen.

Now you should go back and read the chapter "I Just Got Saved, Now What?" and you will find what your next step will be. Congratulations again!

Please feel free to visit our website at www.ReachingMillionsMinistries.com and share with us your decision to accept Christ as your personal Savior—a decision that will affect your entire life forever. The best decision you will ever make in your life is to give your life to Christ. When you change, your entire world changes. Welcome into the wonderful light of Jesus!

My Personal Deliverance by God from My Adversary

I want to finish this book by sharing a very personal experience I had in February of 2016. A lot of people may not be able to understand, but I pray that you remember how the Lord came to my rescue and know that He will do the same for you if you allow Him to in your time of trouble.

I was invited out of state to preach a three-day Revival Service. On the second night of the service, a young man gave his life to the Lord—not just any young man but a man whose mother told me was called from birth to preach and teach the Word of God but had strayed into the world of drugs, etc.

After another night of Revival Service, where the presence of the Lord was manifested and felt throughout the sanctuary, I returned home, but not without a spiritual battle. A natural storm formed and forced my flight to be canceled several times. Then, for no reason that the airline could explain, my seat was changed, and I went from seat 2A to seat 32. This change did not matter to me because I realized that God had a financial blessing for me (in the form of a refund for the ticket I'd originally purchased). So only a financial gain!

Finally, instead of getting back home at 9 p.m., I arrived home close to midnight. Then for the first time in my traveling life (over thirty-seven plus years), I had to wait for my luggage to arrive on another flight. Nevertheless, God returned me home safely.

However, I knew something was wrong. I could feel the attack but didn't know what it was or in what area it was coming. So, I prayed and asked two very anointed men of God to pray for me as well.

After they prayed for me, I could see a brighter light. Still, I could feel something trying to pull me down. God spoke to one of the men who was praying for me and revealed what the devil was trying to push me down into a place of frustration. Well, the next day after they prayed, it seemed to worsen, and I became very agitated and frustrated about the simple things. At the end of the day, I knew that this was for sure a great spiritual battle and that I needed the Lord as never before. You know, sometimes a daughter just needs her Daddy to show up!

When something starts to alter your character, you had better know that you need to get to the Lord and get into His arms of protection quickly. Around evening, I heard the Lord speak to me and say, "Retreat." I realized that this meant to back up and let the Lord fight my battle. Stop trying to go on your strength or your past experiences; totally rely on the empowerment of God. God knows when to step in and when to allow you to move forward on the battlefield with full determination to defeat the devil in Jesus' name, but then it was time for me to "Retreat." You must know where your safe haven is within your household. Mine was my bedroom, for that's where I seek the Lord and pray and listen for Him to answer and show me what to do and how to do it. The devil was defeated on Calvary, and right then, I needed to go back to the cross and "Retreat."

I finally fell asleep in my room while resting peacefully in my lounge chair. The next thing I remembered was that it was past midnight. I transferred to my bed. God woke me up around 3 a.m. and told me to pray. I could not believe it, but the thing (prayer) that has always come easily for me and has been done with tremendous joy and excitement from my heart was now a battle within me. Then it was bought back to me by the Spirit of God, Romans 8:26 (KJV): "Likewise the Spirit also helpeth our infirmities: for we know not what we should pray for as we ought: but the Spirit itself maketh intercession for us with groanings which cannot be uttered." So, I started to pray by the Holy Spirit. I remember that my hands were up in the air, and I was calling on the name of Jesus. I continued to say, "Jesus, Jesus, and Jesus" over and over again.

My Personal Deliverance by God from My Adversary (Continued)

The next thing I remembered was that I could see fiery darts being fired at me as if they were coming from a machine gun (spiritual insight). I could feel myself trying to stand, yet seeing things on my right and left grabbing my arms and trying to bring me down. Then, a light so bright and big that it blinded me enveloped me like arms and picked me up. I will never be able to totally explain it to you, but when the light showed up, I knew it was the Lord because my enemies quickly started to tremble, and they all scattered. They ran in all different ways. There were so many enemies that I could not count them. They scattered to the left, right, and in front of me, just running scared and very quickly.

Now, that same light enveloped me in His arms and ascended with me. He took me to a high place and told me to "soar." I realized that this was the Lord and that He had delivered me from the snare of the devil.

People, you need to know that God is real and also that the devil is real. However, once you accept Jesus as your Lord and Savior, then you have full authority over all of the devil's power.

> Then the seventy returned with joy, saying, 'Lord, even the demons are subject to us in Your name.' And He said to them, 'I saw Satan fall like lightning from heaven. Behold, I give you the authority to trample

on serpents and scorpions, and over all the power of the enemy, and nothing shall by any means hurt you.'

Luke 10:17–19 (NKJV)

God gave me this scripture in the early 1980s, and I am so thankful that He did.

When I got up the next morning to get on our prayer line, which the Lord told me to start in 2011, my entire inner being had been renewed—changed. My prayer was now spoken and prayed with great assurance. I had never felt like this before. While we were praying, the power of God fell upon that line and allowed me to pray with the power and authority of my Lord and Savior, Jesus Christ. That day, I realized that God had come to my rescue early that morning and had delivered me for certain.

Therefore, when you find yourself in a place (physical or spiritual) that you find very hard, and you are unsure of how to get out, remember my personal experience, which I am sharing with you, and know without a doubt that nothing can attack you from which the Lord will not deliver you out of. Remember to call on Jesus, for at that name, everything must bow, in heaven, on earth, and beneath the earth.

When dark clouds of doubt begin to gather, hit "Scriptural Replay," and listen intently to the following recorded word:

> That at the name of Jesus every knee should bow, of *things* in heaven, and *things* in earth, and *things* under the earth; And *that* every tongue should confess that Jesus Christ *is* Lord, to the glory of God the Father.
>
> Philippians 2:10–12 (KJV)

My Personal Deliverance by God from My Adversary (Continued)

I pray that you were truly blessed by reading this book. This book came to pass from my love for God and His people. Through my experience of writing this book, I finally understand the true meaning of what Jesus says in Luke 4:18–19:

> The Spirit of the Lord is upon me, because he hath anointed me to preach the gospel to the poor; he hath sent me to heal the brokenhearted, to preach deliverance to the captives, and recovering of sight to the blind, to set at liberty them that are bruised, To preach the acceptable year of the Lord.
>
> Luke 4:18–19 (KJV)

There is no doubt at all that the Spirit of the Lord was upon me while writing this book. Please know that God loves you so much that He interrupted my life to have me write this book for His people. So please don't just read it once, but constantly refer to it as a help in your everyday life. I can assure you that God did not have me stop with this first book. You can look forward to more to come!

I leave you with 1 John 4:8 (KJV), "He that loveth not knoweth not God; for God is love."

Encouraging Scriptures to Read Daily

All taken from the King James Bible

> And thou shalt love the Lord thy God with all thy heart, and with all thy soul, and with all thy mind, and with all thy strength: this *is* the first commandment.
>
> Mark 12:30

> *And* having spoiled principalities and powers, he made a shew of them openly, triumphing over them in it.
>
> Colossians 2:15

> Peace I leave with you, my peace I give unto you: not as the world giveth, give I unto you. Let not your heart be troubled, neither let it be afraid.
>
> John 14:27

> Trust in the LORD with all thine heart; and lean not unto thine own understanding. In all thy ways acknowledge him, and he shall direct thy paths.
>
> Proverbs 3:5–6

> And the seventy returned again with joy, saying, Lord, even the devils are subject unto us through thy name. And he said unto them, I beheld Satan as lightning fall

from heaven. Behold, I give unto you power to tread on serpents and scorpions, and over all the power of the enemy: and nothing shall by any means hurt you. Notwithstanding in this rejoice not, that the spirits are subject unto you; but rather rejoice, because your names are written in heaven.

Luke 10:17–20

About the Author

If you would like more detailed information about the author, Penny L. Grace, please visit our website:
www.ReachingMillionsMinistries.com

CPSIA information can be obtained
at www.ICGtesting.com
Printed in the USA
LVHW081753290322
714729LV00013BA/405